Revealing the Heart of a Servant

A Study of Mark

Wes and Elaine Willis

ACCENT PUBLICATIONS
Colorado Springs, Colorado

Accent Publications
4050 Lee Vance View
P.O. Box 36640
Colorado Springs, Colorado 80936

Printed in the United States of America

Library of Congress catalog Card Number 94-71165
ISBN 0-89636-308-2

Second Printing

CONTENTS

Introduction to Mark

What characterizes Mark's Gospel? If you were to ask two people to describe the same event, their accounts probably would differ. Neither necessarily would be wrong, but each would emphasize those aspects that proved most interesting to that observer. Our backgrounds, previous experiences, temperaments, personal interest, and countless other elements influence us. They determine what we see and how we perceive any given set of circumstances.

Each of the Gospel writers was a unique individual too. And the Holy Spirit guided each writer, with his own personal perspective, to record Christ's life from that vantage point. Mark's style is active, alive, emphatic. He wrote much of the narrative using the present tense. This gives his narrative a sense of action and immediacy. In fact many narratives begin with the word "immediately," which contributes to the feeling of action. And we often encounter narratives strung together with few connectives or logical transitions.

Who was Mark? We don't know for sure, but we do know that he was not one of the 12 Apostles. He does not identify himself in the text, but that doesn't mean we are completely in the dark. He probably was John Mark, Barnabas' cousin, who accompanied Paul and Barnabas on their first missionary trip. But when it came time for the second trip, Paul took Silas, and Barnabas took Mark. Mark probably wrote his Gospel before the other three, perhaps as early as A.D. 57 or 58. In fact the other Gospel writers well may have relied on Mark's account in compiling their records.

Mark may have been the son of an early believer. Perhaps he was too young to be a disciple, but followed and listened to Jesus whenever possible. It is likely that Mark was a close friend of the Apostle Peter. He probably gathered much of his information from Peter, and then supplemented it with other verbal and written accounts, as well as from his own observation.

It is most important for us to recognize that, in whatever way Mark gathered his information, the Holy Spirit infused the process—guiding, directing, and protecting the record from error. Mark's Gospel provides us with an accurate picture of Jesus Christ, the Suffering Servant. Jesus served through His life and He served through His death. May we gain a deeper understanding of who Jesus is, and of how we should live and serve as His representatives.

❖

1

The Beginning of Jesus' Ministry
MARK 1:1–45

❖

Someone once asked a great orchestra conductor which was the most difficult instrument to play. The maestro's immediate response was, "Second fiddle." He went on to explain that everyone wants to play first chair, but the supporting roles are equally important. An orchestra comprised of only first chair players would be absurd.

When our sons began playing soccer, we observed the same dynamics at work on the soccer field. Every player wanted to score goals. That was the glory position. The coaches tried to explain that competent defensive players were every bit as important as the forwards. In fact, if the defense is strong enough, a team needs only one goal per game to finish with an undefeated season. But immature players don't buy that. They've watched too many games on television, and listened to too many athletes who talk about being number one. They don't want to play second fiddle.

John the Baptist's ministry was playing second fiddle. His job was to announce the Messiah. And John did this with all of his energy. He called Israel to repent and prepare for the kingdom of God. And John was faithful, even to the point of prison and death. He understood that faithfulness to God's call was more important than being number one. Each of us needs to recognize that our mission in life is to point others to "Number One"—to Jesus Christ. We all play second fiddle. May we do it to the glory of God.

JOHN PREPARES THE WAY FOR JESUS (Mark 1:1–13)

I*t must have been some sight. John, a rugged outdoorsman, was preaching to multitudes in the wilderness. And as they confessed their sins, he baptized them, calling them to prepare for the Messiah, whom he also baptized.

1. (1:1) *What clues can you find that give you some idea of the contents of Mark's gospel?*

2. (1:2–3) *According to these verses quoted from Isaiah 40:3, what was the task of one preparing the way for the Messiah?*

3. (1:4–8) *John obviously understood the job he had been sent to do. What was his message? (See also Luke 1:36, 63.)*

❒ *How did the people respond when they saw John? How do you think his dress and behavior affected their reception of his message?*

4. (1:12–13) *Just as Christ faced temptation, spiritual leaders also do today. What kinds of temptation might a lay or professional spiritual leader encounter?*

JESUS BEGINS HIS MINISTRY (Mark 1:14–20)

Few of us would go to the seashore to recruit the key leaders for Christianity. And yet Jesus did just that. He called Peter, Andrew, James, and John to leave their nets and follow Him.

1. (1:14–15) *The Jews understood Jesus' proclamation of the kingdom of God to be the long–awaited reign of the Messiah. The messianic kingdom, a period of justice and righteousness, was prophesied in Isaiah 11:1–11; Micah 4:6–8, and Zechariah 9:9–10. What was the emphasis of Jesus' message when He preached "the gospel of the kingdom of God"?*

2. (1:16–18) *What do you think Simon (Peter) and Andrew understood Jesus was calling them to do?*

❒ *How did they respond?*

3. (1:19–20) *According to Mark, what did it mean for James and John to follow Jesus?*

JESUS TEACHES AND HEALS MANY (Mark 1:21–34)

Jesus was different from anyone the Jews had ever seen. Unlike other teachers, Jesus taught with *authority.* He could heal with just a word, and even the demonic forces of evil cowered before Him.

1. (1:21–22) *The scribes specialized in studying and teaching the Mosaic Law (both the written Law and the oral interpretation of the Law) and in judging matters of Law. How did Jesus' teaching contrast with those teachers?*

❒ *Why do you think people responded with astonishment?*

2. (1:23–26) *What significance do you see in the response of the possessed man?*

❒ *Who really spoke to Jesus through the possessed man in the synagogue? Wasn't he out of place in a house of God?*

3. (1:27) *Why did the people in the synagogue react with amazement? What do their questions reveal?*

4. (1:29–34) *Mark's Gospel reveals Jesus as the Servant-Saviour. How did Jesus' ministries in the area around Capernaum reflect His servanthood?*

❒ *Why do you think Jesus did not permit the demons to speak and reveal who He was?*

JESUS SUFFERS THE STRESS OF FAME (Mark 1:35–45)

Many people think that it would be great to be famous. Yet Jesus was so pressured that He had to steal away to get any private time—even to pray. And still they found Him. So He returned and taught, healed and ministered.

1. (1:35) *What time of day did Jesus get away to be alone?*

❒ *Where did He go?*

❒ *Why did He do this?*

❒ *How is this an example for us today?*

2. (1:37–39) *What was the real focus or purpose of Jesus' ministry?*

3. (1:41) *How did Jesus respond to the leper and why was this unusual?*

❒ *What does Jesus' response to the "unclean" teach us about our ministry?*

4. (1:43–45) *What did Jesus command the healed leper to do? (Note Jesus' respect for the regulations of the Mosaic Law [Leviticus 14:1–20] regarding the cleansing of a leper.)*

❒ *The devils, verse 34, obeyed Jesus. The man, verse 45, did not. What made the difference in their responses?*

❐ *What were the consequences of the leper's actions?*

DIGGING DEEPER

1. *In what ways might you have a ministry similar to that of John the Baptist?*

2. *What might it cost you to follow Jesus today?*

3. *Mark gives no details about Jesus' temptation in the wilderness, although Matthew 4:1–11 and Luke 4:1– 13 provide a more complete account of the temptations. How is this consistent with the position of a servant? How could Jesus' example help you handle temptations in your daily life?*

4. *Jesus experienced stress as He ministered. What stress do you experience because you serve Him?*

❐ *How should you deal with those pressures?*

❖

2

Varied Responses to Jesus

MARK 2:1—3:19

❖

Ordinarily, people don't like to be criticized. Most of us enjoy praise, and we want to be recognized for doing a good job, so it can be painful when we are told what we did wrong. Students prefer to know how many questions they answered correctly on a test rather than how many they missed. When we perform an assignment at work, it is gratifying to hear what an excellent job we did, and it's much less pleasant when the evaluation is, "Let me explain why your performance didn't measure up."

But as we gain confidence, mature individuals seek negative as well as positive evaluations. True growth comes only as a result of recognizing both. A competent worker seeks analysis of weak performances so that those areas can be strengthened. An athlete will spend hours analyzing the details of a performance, perhaps reviewing a videotape repeatedly to discover any flaws.

The ability to handle negative as well as positive feedback is a sign of maturity. Healthy, well–balanced individuals can face both kinds. But no matter how mature a person becomes, invalid criticism is always hard to accept. Invalid criticism is the kind of criticism that Jesus had to endure.

Though both His actions and His attitudes were faultless, Jesus was criticized and condemned by those who knew better. In fact, it was *because* of the good He did, especially healing the sick, that the religious leaders lay in wait for Him. They took every opportunity to find fault and even began plotting how they could have Him killed.

AMAZEMENT OF THE PEOPLE (Mark 2:1–12)

There is a saying that actions speak louder than words. In Jesus' case, both His words and His actions spoke loudly. People were amazed, not only by His teaching but by the miracles and wonders He performed.

1. (2:1–2) *Word spread rapidly that Jesus was at a certain house in Capernaum. How do you think people knew where Jesus was ministering?*

2. (2:3–4) *How did the paralyzed man and his friends demonstrate their faith?*

❒ *Whose faith resulted in the healing?*

3. (2:6–7) *Blasphemy is sin directed toward God in which a person demeans or makes light of God and His power or claims rights belonging only to God. Why did the teachers of the Law conclude that Jesus was blaspheming?*

4. (2:9) *What answer would you give to Jesus' question? Why?*

❒ *Do you think Jesus expected an answer to His question? If so, which answer do you think He expected?*

5. (2:10–11) *What did Jesus' ability to heal the paralytic indicate about His authority to forgive sins?*

6. (2:12, 2:6–7) *Compare the people's response with the scribes' response. Why did the people respond differently?*

CRITICISM OF JESUS AND HIS DISCIPLES (Mark 2:13–22)

Though many people were praising Jesus, others were looking for any mistakes. No matter what Jesus did, someone seemed to be there to find fault with something. They even criticized His choice of companions and His disciples' eating habits.

1. (2:13–14) *Tax collectors were among the most despised and hated persons in Jewish society. They were usually Jews who worked for the Roman government. They were allowed to add their own collection fees (usually very large) to the tax bill. Why would Levi (Matthew) leave his lucrative position to follow Jesus?*

2. (2:15-16) *Why would sinners and publicans follow Jesus?*

❐ *To the Pharisees, the word sinners referred to anyone who did not keep the details of the Pharisaic traditions and regulations. How did Jesus violate their traditions and regulations? Why did the Pharisees criticize and condemn Jesus?*

3. (2:17) *What did Jesus mean by His response to the Pharisees?*

4. (2:18–20) *One of the Pharisees' strict traditions was to fast on Monday and Thursday, even though the Mosaic Law commanded fasting only on the Day of Atonement (Leviticus 16:29–34). Why did Christ's disciples not fast as the disciples of the Pharisees and of John did?*

❒ *In the illustration of the "bridegroom" (the guests), and the "feasting," whom does the bridegroom represent and whom do the children of the bridechamber represent?*

5. (2:21–22) *Jesus seemed to be using these two parables to indicate that the old system (the Mosaic Law and the Pharisaic traditions) and the new system (Jesus' gospel of the kingdom) could not be mixed together. Today, if a person accepts Jesus' teaching, what characteristics of his/her old religion and lifestyle might change radically? (See Philippians 3:4–11.)*

CONFLICT OVER SABBATH OBSERVANCE (Mark 2:23—3:6)

Politics does make strange bedfellows. In this case, the Pharisees who were threatened by Jesus' religious power, and the Herodians who worried about His political influence, forged an alliance in order to plot Jesus' death.

1. (2:23-24, 3:2) *Why were the Pharisees watching Jesus so closely?*

2. (2:25, 3:4) *Jesus did nothing forbidden in the Mosaic Law, but He seems to have ignored the petty regulations of the Pharisaic interpretations of the Law. What irony did Jesus point out when He was criticized by the Pharisees?*

❒ **(3:4)** *Why did the Pharisees remain silent when Jesus questioned them about doing good and healing on the Sabbath?*

3. (3:5–6) *Jesus' anger seems to have been directed toward the Pharisees' stubborn reaction to His claim and substantiation of being the Messiah. How did the Pharisees seem to feel when Jesus healed the man with the withered hand?*

❒ *How should they have responded?*

❒ *What did the Pharisees do after this confrontation with Jesus?*

POPULAR ACCEPTANCE OF JESUS (Mark 3:7–19)

In spite of the criticism and opposition of the leaders, people flocked to see Jesus. No doubt most people were only curious; some may have shown allegiance to Jesus. But Jesus selected twelve of the many following Him to be special disciples—His apostles.

1. (3:7–10) *People came from as far as Idumea (approximately 120 miles to the south) and Sidon (about 50 miles to the northwest) to see Jesus. What was it about Jesus that attracted so many people?*

2. (3:10–12) *What is similar here to 1:21-26? What is revealed here about Jesus' authority?*

3. (3:14–15) *What were Jesus' expectations for the twelve disciples whom He chose to become apostles?*

4. (3:16–17,19) *Mark adds specific details about some apostles. Who are they and what did he add? Why do you think they received special recognition?*

DIGGING DEEPER

1. *It is obvious that the paralytic was transformed by his contact with Jesus (2:1–12). In what ways does Jesus change people's lives today?*

❒ *What difference does Jesus make in your daily life?*

❒ *Which of these changes can be seen by those around you?*

2. *In what ways might someone today elevate humanly conceived traditions and regulations above a genuine concern to meet the needs of others and to alleviate their suffering?*

3. *Jesus shared meals with those who needed His message (2:16–17). What ways do you befriend and reach out to those around you who need to believe His message today?*

❖

3

Jesus Explains the Kingdom of God

MARK 3:20—4:34

❖

Most of us have too many things to do and not enough time to do them. We juggle our daily activities, family, work, friendships, exercise, and hobbies. Countless other good activities demand our time. It seems as though we are spread so thin that at times we must be transparent. We want to cry out, "Stop! Just stop everything and let me catch up!"

Even Jesus faced the demands and pressures of an active lifestyle. His family was concerned that He was so busy He didn't even have time to eat. And He *needed* to spend time with His friends and associates. But people constantly demanded His attention—to heal, to teach, and to answer questions. His time was not His own. But through it all, Jesus never lost sight of His goal—to preach the kingdom of God.

This section of Scripture is often called "the Busy Day"—a classic understatement if ever there was one. As you work through this study, remember that Jesus understands your time pressures. Why not pray and ask Him to give you the wisdom to keep all of your obligations and activities in balance? Ask Him to help you decide how to assign priorities to various demands. Then you will be able to distinguish between activities which may all be good but not of equal importance.

JESUS ACCUSED OF SATANIC POWER (Mark 3:20–30)

How do you feel when someone misunderstands you? Jesus was grossly misunderstood by the religious leaders who not only rejected His message, but actually accused Him of healing and casting out demons by Satan's power.

1. (3:20–21) *Why did Jesus' friends conclude that He was out of His mind?*

2. (3:22) *The scribes (Pharisees who were teachers of the Law) had come from Jerusalem (about 75 miles to the south) to evaluate and critique all that Jesus said and did. What was their accusation?*

3. (3:23–26) *The Pharisees had to admit that Jesus had more than human power. But they rejected God as the source of His power and that left only Satan. How did Jesus logically refute their accusations?*

4. (3:27) *What was the second argument that Jesus used to refute the false accusations?*

❒ *Who was the strong man that had to be bound, and what was the "house"? What does this mean?*

5. (3:28-30) *What does Jesus say about sin and forgiveness in these verses?*

JESUS IDENTIFIES HIS TRUE FAMILY (Mark 3:31–35)

Jesus' earthly family was physically related to Him, but any of us can become members of His spiritual family through our spiritual relationship to Him. This relationship is just as real as any physical ties.

1. (3:31–33) *Why do you think that Jesus' mother and brothers called for Him?*

❒ *What was Jesus' rhetorical question given in reply to those who told Him that His family was there?*

2. (3:34–35) *What is Jesus' requirement to be included in His family?*

❒ *What does that mean?*

❒ *In what ways does Jesus' response broaden the usual concept of family?*

THE PARABLE OF THE SOWER (Mark 4:1–20)

Everyone loves a good story, and Jesus' followers were no exception. Parables are one of the basic methods that Jesus used in teaching. One definition of a parable is, "an earthly story with a heavenly meaning." A parable has physical or "story" elements. But in a parable these elements have been carefully chosen to represent spiritual truths also. To interpret a parable, look for the spiritual parallels to the main points of the story, but not necessarily in every detail. The Parable of the Sower is one of Jesus' best-known and most-detailed parables.

1. (4:1–9,14-20) *This first parable describes the spiritual kingdom of God. The main "story" elements are listed below. To the right of each "story" element, write out the "spiritual" meaning of that element. (You may also want to look at Matthew 13:3–8 and Luke 8:5–15.)*

Sower (farmer) —

Seed—

Way side (path) —

Fowls of the air (birds) —

Stony ground —

Sun —

Thorns —

Good ground —

Bountiful crop —

2. (4:10–12) *In one or two short sentences, summarize the Parable of the Sower.*

❒ *Who were the ones who understood the parables and who were "them that are without"?*

3. (4:15–20) *Why do people respond so differently to the Word of God?*

THREE MORE KINGDOM PARABLES (Mark 4:21–34)

*B*uilding on the truths He had revealed in the Parable of the Sower, Jesus continued to explain through parables the nature of the kingdom. Through the Parables of the Lamp, the Growing Seed, and the Mustard Seed, Jesus taught that His kingdom is a spiritual kingdom, not an earthly, physical one.

1. (4:21–22) *How is the Word of God like a light?*

2. (4:23) *What does God's exhortation in this verse mean?*

3. (4:24–25) *Summarize in your own words what the warning contained here might mean to people today.*

4. (4:26–29) *In what ways is the truth about the kingdom of God like the seeds described in the Parable of the Growing Seed?*

5. (4:30–32) *The seed analogy is continued in the Parable of the Mustard Seed. An annual shrub, in a matter of weeks it grows from a tiny seed to a large bush (10–12 feet high). What features of this parable explain the growth of the spiritual kingdom of God?*

DIGGING DEEPER

1. *The Pharisees rejected Jesus, going so far as to credit His power to Satan. What are some of the excuses that people give today for rejecting Jesus?*

2. *Are you a member of Jesus' spiritual family? On what do you base this conclusion?*

3. *What activities and attitudes do you share with your physical family and what parallels to these do you see in your relationship to your spiritual family?*

Physical	*Spiritual Parallels*

4. *Based on your response to the Word of God, which type of ground are you?*

❒ *What fruit are you bearing, and would you describe it as 30–, 60– or 100–fold abundance?*

❖

Jesus' Power-Filled Ministry

MARK 4:35—6:6

❖

Those of us who live in major metropolitan areas often forget the personal nature of small towns. Recently, while visiting with relatives who live in a *very* small town, we discussed the "fun" items listed in their newspaper. It is common to find "news articles" about those who just returned from vacation, how long they were there, and what they did. Visiting out–of–town guests are of interest and announced in the newspaper. People in small towns want to know what is happening to their friends and neighbors.

Such is the kind of town that Jesus came from. Surely a few townspeople must have expressed some "small-town-boy-makes-good" pride in Jesus as He began His ministry. Yet there is another side to small-town life.

Although some people walked more than a hundred miles to hear Him teach or to be healed, when Jesus tried to minister in and around His hometown, people were skeptical. "How could He do these wondrous things? He is just the son of the carpenter." "Where could He have gotten such wisdom? We know His brothers and sisters, and they are just common people." Because of their lack of faith, Jesus could not minister to those who had lived in closest proximity to Him in the early years of His life.

JESUS' POWER OVER THE WEATHER (Mark 4:35–41)

Everybody talks about the weather, but nobody does anything about it. At least not until Jesus came along. In the midst of a ferocious storm on the Sea of Galilee, the disciples were overwhelmed. But Jesus awoke and showed that His power was that of the Creator.

1. (4:37–39) *Sudden, furious storms often arose without warning on Galilee. In this storm, even seasoned fishermen—skilled boatmen—were afraid they were going to die. Why do you think that Jesus was asleep in the stern of the boat?*

❒ *How could His being asleep have been part of Jesus' plan for training the disciples?*

2. (4:39, 41) *What do these verses indicate about Jesus' power?*

❒ *What do verses 38 and 41 tell us about the disciples' understanding of Jesus?*

3. (4:40-41) *"Fearful" comes from a word meaning "to be timid" or "cowardly," while "feared exceedingly" has a literal meaning of, "were afraid with great fear." It meant "to dread" or "to revere." What was the difference between the disciples' fear during the storm and their fear after the storm?*

JESUS' POWER OVER SATAN (Mark 5:1–20)

The demoniac was the talk of the town—he was their horrible badge of notoriety. In fact, the townspeople were so upset when Jesus freed the demoniac that they asked Jesus to leave their area.

1. (5:1–5) *This event took place in a predominantly Gentile area (Gadara) on the eastern shore of Galilee. What characterized the demoniac?*

2. (5:7–9) *Who spoke to Jesus through the man?*

3. (5:10–12) *Why do you think they requested what they did?*

4. (5:13) *The word "legion" meant 6,000 when it referred to a division of Roman soldiers. Figuratively, legion could mean "many" or "powerful." What happened to the demons when they left the man?*

5. (5:14–17) *Why would the local inhabitants apparently place a higher value on their pigs than upon the human being who was delivered from Satan's domination?*

❐ *What would you have expected their response to be?*

6. (5:18–20) *What did the man want to do, and what did Jesus tell him to do instead?*

❐ *How is this similar to or different from Jesus' confrontation with the demons in 1:21-28 and 3:11-12?*

JESUS' POWER OVER SICKNESS AND DEATH (Mark 5:21–43)

*E*ven though the Gadarenes didn't want Jesus around, others did. After recrossing the Sea of Galilee, Jesus was thronged by those who wanted to be healed. On the way to heal Jairus' daughter, a woman touched Jesus coat and was healed. Then Jesus raised Jairus' daughter from the dead.

1. (5:22–23) *Jairus was not a Pharisee, but he was a leader in the synagogue. Perhaps he had met or seen Jesus when He first ministered in Capernaum (cf. Mark 1:21–28). What was unusual in Jairus approaching Jesus?*

2. (5:25–26) *Why did the woman come to Jesus?*

3. (5:30–31) *Jesus knows what is in the heart of every person, so He obviously knew who had touched Him. Yet, He gave the woman the opportunity to identify herself. What did Jesus mean when He said that "virtue" had gone out of Him?*

4. (5:28,34) *What cured the woman?*

❒ *In light of Jesus' teaching in Mark 3:33-35, why would Jesus address this woman (5:34) as "Daughter"? What does this suggest about His relationship to His followers?*

5. (5:35-36) *What happened to Jairus' daughter during the delay?*

❒ *What did the men announcing the news indicate about their understanding of Jesus?*

❒ *What did Jesus tell Jairus?*

❒ *How can you apply that message to your life?*

6. (5:38–40) *How did the people respond to Jesus before He raised the girl?*

7. *What insights about Jesus are revealed through His behavior in these two events?*

JESUS' POWER NEUTRALIZED (Mark 6:1–6)

Though Jesus had power over nature, illness, and even death, He did not force people to accept Him. Where He was rejected, He was unable to minister.

1. (6:1–3) *The people in Jesus' hometown recognized that Jesus' works were mighty and that He was wise. Why did they reject Jesus, even to the point of being offended by Him?*

2. (6:4–6) *Why was Jesus unable to do many miracles in Nazareth?*

DIGGING DEEPER

1. *All of the people in this passage could observe Jesus' miracles and listen to His teaching. Some believed. Some did not. What made the difference? What attitudes were evident in each group?*

❒ *Some came to Him to resolve their unsolvable situations. Others were offended. How have you taken the circumstances of your life that could potentially overwhelm and destroy you to Jesus to receive His encouragement and help?*

❒ *How do you think God might be using these experiences to help you grow and mature?*

2. *In what areas of life might we experience conflict between the value of material things (or profit) and the value of people (human life)?*

❒ *What results might we see in our personal or vocational lives if we really value people above things and/or profit?*

3. *Jesus showed great compassion both to the chronically ill woman and to Jairus' family. When in your life have you experienced God's great compassion and understanding?*

❒ *How are you sharing the news of God's compassion and power with others you meet?*

❖

Jesus Trains His Disciples

MARK 6:7–56

❖

Do you ever have trouble identifying people whom you haven't seen for some time? Many of us can recognize faces but struggle to remember names. It seems that meeting people in a location where we don't expect to see them confuses most of us.

Jesus constantly encountered people who did not recognize Him—people who speculated about His identity and who suggested some very diverse explanations of who He was and where He came from. Some thought He was Elijah; others suggested He was another of the prophets. Herod thought Jesus was John the Baptist whom he had executed. Even Jesus' disciples were confused. But this was soon to change, for Jesus' mission was reaching a crucial turning point.

TWELVE APOSTLES SENT TO PREACH (Mark 6:7–13,30–31)

By this point in Jesus' ministry, the disciples have matured to the point where 12 of them are able to minister on their own. Now Jesus commissions them to go out and preach the gospel of the kingdom.

1. (6:7) *What authority (power) did Jesus give the apostles?*

❒ *Why? What were they to do? What message were they to preach? (See 6:12.)*

❒ *How did their authority validate the message they were proclaiming?*

2. (6:8–11) *Special conditions seemed to apply to this particular assignment only. The extra tunic was used as a night covering which would not be needed if they were given hospitality. What response would demonstrate that some had received the apostles and their message?*

❐ *What were the apostles to do if they were not received? What did that mean?*

3. (6:13) *What ministries did the apostles have in addition to preaching?*

4. (6:30–31) *What did the apostles do after their assignments were completed?*

❐ *How might this pattern be followed for those in ministry today?*

HEROD AND JOHN THE BAPTIST (Mark 6:14–29)

It's amazing what guilt can do to a person. After having John executed, Herod was consumed with guilt and fear for what he had done. He even feared that Jesus was John resurrected.

1. (6:14–28) *These verses introduce a flashback that describes the circumstances surrounding Herod's execution of John. What did Herod assume about Jesus when he heard of Him?*

❐ *Why did Herod have such a guilty conscience?*

2. (6:26) *The text says Herod was sorry—yet he murdered John the Baptist anyway. Why was he sorry and why did he go through with it?*

JESUS FEEDS FIVE THOUSAND (Mark 6:32–44)

At one time or another, most of us have felt overwhelmed by people. Apparently Jesus felt the same way and tried to get away. But when Jesus and His disciples reached a solitary "desert place," thousands of people were waiting. And not only did Jesus teach and heal them, but He fed them too—with only a little boy's lunch.

1. (6:31–33) *Why was Jesus ministering in a remote place?*

2. (6:33) *People saw where Jesus was headed and apparently followed the shoreline to meet Him. How do you think Jesus felt when He saw a crowd waiting and what did He do?*

❒ *How do you respond when you "need your own space" and can't get it?*

3. (6:35–36) *What problem did the disciples observe?*

4. (6:36–38) *What is the difference between the disciples' solution and Jesus'?*

5. (6:39–44) *Most likely the loaves were similar to small rolls and the fish were a small variety that was smoked or salted. What was Jesus really demonstrating:*

- *to the crowd*

- *to the disciples*

- *to us?*

JESUS WALKS ON WATER (Mark 6:45–56)

This was quite a day for the disciples. After the miraculous feeding, Jesus sent them back across the lake in a small boat. But because of another fierce storm, they struggled at sea all nigh. Completely exhausted, they were overcome with fear when Jesus approached, walking on the water. But through this experience, Jesus taught them another lesson.

1. (6:45–47) *Why did Jesus send His disciples ahead of Him?*

❐ *How do you think they felt about this?*

2. (6:48) *Jesus saw the disciples struggling at sunset and yet waited to come to them until the fourth watch (between 3:00 and 6:00 a.m.) Why do you think that Jesus waited so long before coming to His disciples?*

❐ *How do you think that God may employ a similar strategy to teach us lessons today?*

3. (6:49-51) *The disciples were terrified when they saw Jesus approaching them, walking on the water. Why, and how did Jesus calm their fears?*

4. (6:52) *This verse states that the disciples "considered not the miracle of the loaves." What was it that they did not understand?*

5. (6:53–56) *What was the attitude of the people in the area and how did they respond?*

DIGGING DEEPER

1. *God used miracles to validate the message that the apostles proclaimed, "Repent, Messiah is here." What in your life gives credibility to the truth of God's Word that you share with others?*

2. *What does Jesus feeding 5,000 with only a small lunch suggest about His use of you and your resources?*

❒ *How should we respond when we recognize opportunities to serve?*

❒ *What specific resources (possessions, talents, interests, opportunities), which may seem insignificant to you, do you have that God could use to serve Him?*

3. *In what areas might you be insensitive to Jesus and what He wants you to do?*

❒ *How could you increase your sensitivity to those in your family?*

At work?

At church?

❖

Jesus Ministers to People
MARK 7:1—8:26

❖

*T*hink back to a time when you were misunderstood. Can you recall the circumstances surrounding the misunderstanding? Remember how you felt and what you did to correct the situation. Were you able to resolve the problem or did your efforts only make things worse? You may have attempted to make a humorous comment. But instead of being perceived as charming and witty, the people around you thought your contribution was inappropriate or stupid. Their opinions were obvious from their reactions. When you tried to explain your intentions, the misunderstanding only increased.

Even though He always responded appropriately, Jesus also lived with misunderstanding. The Pharisees constantly judged and condemned Him. They made every conceivable accusation against Him. Even His disciples misunderstood Him. But Jesus remained patient and loving. He repeatedly explained what His followers should have understood. We can be sure that Jesus understands what we feel when we are misunderstood. And He stands ready to support and comfort us in our most difficult moments.

RITUALS OR REAL WORSHIP? (Mark 7:1–23)

One of the regulations of the Pharisaic tradition was the ritual washing before a meal. Many of their ritualistic regulations focused on external matters. Jesus tried to show them that the internal is more important than the external—the spiritual more important than the physical.

1. (7:1–4) *The Pharisees were notorious for setting up detailed, meticulous regulations for all aspects of life, often obscuring (or ignoring) God's law in the process. Why were the Pharisees criticizing Jesus here?*

2. (7:5) *What did they want Jesus to do?*

3. (7:6–9) *Of what did Jesus accuse the Pharisees?*

❐ *What was the relative significance of the Pharisees' complaint with the significance of Jesus' accusation?*

4. (7:10–13) *One Pharisaic tradition said that if a man declared all his possessions to be "Corban" (dedicated to God), no one else could lay claim to them. How did the Pharisees use this tradition to avoid obligations clearly commanded in God's law?*

5. (7:14–23) *What distinctions did Jesus draw between the physical and the spiritual dimensions of life?*

❐ *What are some of the physical concerns or temporal issues that might occupy our attention and divert us from more important spiritual issues?*

6. (7:17–18) *What was Jesus' analysis of His disciples' condition?*

JESUS HEALS A GIRL AND A MAN (Mark 7:24–37)

Though Jesus had certain ministry patterns, He often varied His approach. In this passage, He first went outside the nation of Israel, and then He healed a deaf and mute man in a rather different manner from His other healings.

1. (7:24) *This miracle in Phoenicia, about 40 miles northwest of Capernaum, shows Jesus reaching out to Gentiles, building on the Jews' growing rejection of Him. Why do you think Jesus wanted to keep His presence from being known?*

2. (7:25-26) *Why did the Syrophenician woman appeal to Jesus for help?*

3. (7:27–29) *Jesus' answer to the woman is in figurative language. What do the various elements represent?*

Children —

Children's bread —

Dogs —

Note: "Dogs" in verse 27 literally means "little dogs." It is a term used of house pets, not outdoor scavengers or wild dogs. Though Gentiles were called dogs by the Jews, in this context it probably was not meant derogatorily.

4. (7:26–30) *Why do you think that Jesus healed the Gentile woman's daughter as she requested? (See Matthew 15:24–28 also.)*

5. (7:31–32) *Why do you think the people brought the man to Jesus near Decapolis? Was it faith, concern, a test, or something else?*

6. (7:33–35) *Why do you think Jesus chose to heal in this manner?*

7. (7:36–37) *What did Jesus command the people to do and what did they do instead?*

❐ *Why do you think Jesus told some not to disclose what He had done?*

JESUS FEEDS FOUR THOUSAND (Mark 8:1–10)

What do you do when too many people come to dinner? Order in pizza, toss another potato into the pot, or throw up your hands in despair? The disciples chose the despair route, but Jesus had another plan—feed them with one lunch.

1. (8:1–3) *This is a similar but different event from the time Jesus fed 5,000 with five loaves and two fish. Why was Jesus concerned about this multitude?*

❒ *It seems strange that the disciples were puzzled about how to feed the thousands. Why do you think that they apparently had forgotten how Jesus fed the five thousand?*

2. (8:5–8) *How much food did Jesus begin with and how much was left over?*

JESUS AND THE PHARISEES (Mark 8:11–21)

Any teacher knows the difficulty of trying to teach when the students are hungry. Jesus was no exception. In this instance, He wanted to teach His disciples about the Pharisees, but the disciples seemed to be preoccupied with their stomachs.

1. (8:11-12) *What did the Pharisees ask for and why did they ask?*

❒ *How did Jesus feel about their question and what did He tell them?*

❒ *The Pharisees had rejected what they had seen and yet were demanding still more proof. What "signs" had Jesus already given them?*

2. (8:14–16) *Yeast is a picture of sin or unbelief. What was Jesus warning His disciples about, and how did they misunderstand Him?*

3. (8:14) *Why do you think the disciples thought that they needed more than one loaf when Jesus had just fed 4,000 with seven and 5,000 with five?*

4. (8:17–21) *In what ways do we demonstrate that we are prone to think as the disciples did?*

Disciples' Thoughts/Fears	Our Thoughts/Fears

HEALING THE BLIND MAN AT BETHSAIDA (Mark 8:22–26)

*T*his healing also differs from how Jesus ordinarily healed. In this instance, He performed a two-stage miracle. Jesus first helped the blind man to gain some vision, and then completed the healing in a second step.

1. **(8:23-24)** *What happened in the first stage of healing the blind man at Bethsaida?*

2. **(8:25)** *There is no indication that the man's faith or Jesus' will to heal him was weak, only that Jesus chose to perform the miracle in two steps. Why might Jesus have chosen to heal in two stages instead of instantly?*

DIGGING DEEPER

1. *In what ways might we become so preoccupied with physical, external matters that we forget the spiritual dimension of life? How can we avoid this tendency?*

❐ *In spite of many demands on His time, Jesus still made time for people. How can you incorporate those same values into your life and relationships this week?*

2. *How might we inappropriately let spiritual commitments, traditions, or rituals interfere with physical, earthly responsibilities, such as to our parents? What can help us to keep the proper balance?*

3. *How does the fact that we know that Jesus is the Son of God (many of His early followers seemed confused about this) help us want to know what He taught, and then to obey Him?*

4. *From your observations, in what way can unbelief (or a single sin) have repercussions in the lives of many (like a little leaven in bread dough)?*

❖

7

Jesus Reveals His Earthly Mission

MARK 8:27—9:50

❖

Some years ago Wes asked one of our sons, who was just entering junior high, what vocation interested him. After puzzling for a few minutes, he responded that he would like to be a senior vice president (which was Wes's title at that time).

We have laughed over this many times. He had no real idea what his Dad did, but he concluded that senior vice president would be a nice choice. Of course, he was too young to realize that leadership has many built-in dangers. While it can be an extremely positive experience, any potential leader must recognize the vulnerability of holding that position. When a leader fails, the repercussions can be far-reaching. Not only does it affect the leader's life and career, it can affect countless others, too.

Ego can ensnare anyone. But for a leader, the struggle with ego and its implications seems to be a much larger issue. Minor success tempts a leader to become infatuated with his or her own ability. And there is always the danger of misleading those who have placed their trust in you. Leaders are responsible for more than just themselves. They also are accountable for those whom they lead.

This passage addresses some typical problems. Jesus was misunderstood regularly. Even at this point in His ministry, most people did not comprehend who He was. Both He and His disciples were in highly visible positions. And they were subject to criticism for all they did. When Jesus' disciples failed, their failures affected many others. Jesus' disciples competed for what they thought were higher positions. In this section of Scripture, Jesus warned His disciples of the solemn responsibility they bore in leading others.

JESUS RECOGNIZED AS MESSIAH (Mark 8:27–38)

*I*t seemed as though every person had his own explanation of who Jesus was. But in this section, it was Peter who finally stated clearly that Jesus was the Messiah. Perhaps this is why the disciples struggled so with Jesus' teaching about His coming death and resurrection.

1. (8:27–28) *The identities suggested here are similar to those in 6:15. Why do you think Jesus asked His disciples, "Whom do men say that I am?"*

2. (8:29) *What was Peter's answer to Jesus' question?*

3. (8:30) *The word Christ means "anointed one," the Messiah for whom the Jews were eagerly waiting. What was Jesus' response to Peter's answer? Why would He say this?*

4. (8:31) *Up until this time in His ministry Jesus had taught in parables (4:33–34). This passage marks a significant transition when Jesus began to speak directly and explicitly about His mission. What things did Jesus begin to teach His disciples?*

5. (8:32) *Why do you think Peter responded as he did to Jesus' teaching about His coming suffering?*

6. (8:33) *Jesus responded strongly to Peter's rebuke. How did Peter's suggestion represent Satan's way of thinking rather than God's plan?*

❒ *Peter had just acknowledged that Jesus was the Christ—the long-awaited Messiah. Why would he presume to rebuke Him?*

7. (8:34–38) *Summarize the main points of Jesus' teaching about the demands of discipleship.*

JESUS REVEALS HIS COMING GLORY (Mark 9:1–13)

*E*ven though he had identified Jesus as the Messiah, Peter certainly was not prepared for the dramatic revelation of Jesus' glory and the appearance of Moses and Elijah. And when he made an inappropriate suggestion, God's response must have increased Peter's anxiety.

1. (9:2-4) *This transfiguration experience is believed by many to be the fulfillment of Jesus' prediction in verse 1. What did Peter, James, and John see on the mountain?*

2. (9:5–6) *In the vision, it is likely that Moses represents the Law, and Elijah represented the prophets, both of which directed Israel to Christ. What was Peter's suggestion, and why do you think he responded as he did?*

3. (9:7) *Who spoke to the three disciples from the cloud and what was the significance of the message?*

4. (9:10-11) *Perhaps Peter thought that at this time Jesus was going to establish His kingdom and assume the throne. According to these verses, how well did the disciples understand this whole event? What were the disciples confused about?*

5. (9:12-13) *What did Jesus say about John the Baptist's role in prophecy? (See also Matthew 17:11-13.)*

JESUS EXPLAINS THE SECRET OF POWER (Mark 9:14–32)

Though the disciples had experienced only limited success in their ministry, they had apparently become quite self–assured. When Jesus healed the demon-possessed boy whom they could not heal, He was able to teach them about the source of power and how they could serve God only through His power.

1. (9:14–18) *The nine disciples not with Jesus on the mountain were involved in this incident. Why were these disciples arguing with the teachers of the law?*

2. (9:17–22) *Satan's power is limited, but its results are negative and ultimately destructive, even to the one he uses. What did the evil spirit regularly do to the young man whom it possessed?*

❒ **(9:19)** *What was Jesus' criticism of those whom He confronted?*

3. (9:23–24) *Perhaps the father's faith had been shaken by the disciples' inability to deliver his son. What requirement did the young man's father have to meet in order for Jesus to heal the young man?*

❒ *In Mark 5:36 Jesus used similar words to Jairus. How would you apply these words of Jesus to your life?*

4. (9:25–27) *In delivering the young man, what did Jesus reveal about His power and about Satan's power?*

Jesus' Power	***Satan's Power***

5. (9:28–29) *The disciples knew Jesus had given them power to cast out demons. What was Jesus' explanation to His disciples as to why they could not heal the young man?*

6. (9:30–32) *Jesus again seeks anonymity. Why?*

❒ *What did Jesus teach His disciples about coming events, and what was their response?*

JESUS EXPLAINS SPIRITUAL VALUES (Mark 9:33–50)

*I*t often seems that many people believe in a distortion of the Golden Rule: "He who owns the gold makes the rules." When the disciples fell into the struggle for power, Jesus explained spiritual values about greatness, about attitudes toward other groups, and about the importance of not being drawn into sinful activities.

1. (9:33–34) *Why were the disciples arguing on the way to Capernaum?*

❒ *What similar issues might Christians argue about today?*

2. (9:35) *What principle of leadership did Jesus explain to resolve the disciples' conflict?*

3. (9:36–37) *How did Jesus' attitude toward children explain and reinforce this principle?*

4. (9:38-41) *What issue(s) do these verses deal with?*

❒ *What do they suggest about the possibility of remaining neutral or noncommittal toward Jesus?*

❒ *Contrast Jesus' attitude with the disciples' attitudes. What application is there in Jesus' words for today's church?*

5. (9:42–50) *This series of parables (overstated for emphasis) convey the seriousness of sin and significance of eternal judgment. Summarize Jesus' teaching about the relative importance of the physical and spiritual—of the temporary and eternal.*

❒ *As salt purifies and preserves, so Jesus intended His followers to be a purifying, preserving element in society. How does Jesus' exhortation to "be at peace with each other" (verse 50) relate to His teaching in verses 33–34 and 38–39?*

DIGGING DEEPER

1. *In what ways could our attitudes and suggestions reflect satanic, rather than godly, goals and values?*

❒ *What can we do to avoid this possibility?*

2. *How can we keep from being presumptuous, as Peter was, so that we do not run ahead of God or suggest actions contrary to His will?*

3. *Jesus taught His disciples (9:35) that spiritual leadership isn't based on power or intimidation. What qualities of godly servanthood do you see in verses 33-50?*

❒ *How should Christians demonstrate Christ-like attitudes toward:*

Leaders —

Children —

Others who also follow Christ—

❖

8

The Final Preparation of Jesus' Disciples

MARK 10:1–52

❖

*I*t never ceases to amaze us how much work is involved in preparing to leave on a trip. We made a combination work/vacation family trip to the West Coast several years ago. We drove thousands of miles, had many enjoyable times together, and visited beautiful parts of the country that we never had seen before.

But it seems as though taking care of details in preparation for an absence of two weeks requires at least four weeks of planning and work. Our oldest son Mark was not going with us on this trip, so we needed to give him instructions for all the things that might happen in our absence. Elaine had prepared many meals for him, but there were also plants to water, mail to collect, newspapers to keep, paper-route arrangements, people to contact, phone messages to save, and other details, *ad infinitum.*

And as our departure time drew near, the pace of instruction and Mark's preparation intensified. We kept remembering other instructions to tell Mark. Finally, all of our preparation came to an end because it was time for us to leave. And we did leave, thinking of still more things that we would like to have done, and wishing that we had just a little more time with our son.

In the Gospel of Mark, a similar dynamic seems to be at work. There is great emphasis throughout this Gospel on how Jesus prepared His disciples for His departure. The intensity seems to reach its peak in this portion of Mark's record (10:1–52). Immediately following Jesus' final preparation of His disciples, the narrative of chapter 11 describes the events of the final week before Jesus' crucifixion.

ATTITUDE TOWARD MARRIAGE AND CHILDREN (Mark 10:1–16)

Some people seem never to learn. The Pharisees refused to give up trying to trick Jesus, even though they came out on the short end every time. In this passage they tried to force Him to take sides in one of their debates. Instead, He taught God's principles and then demonstrated His attitude toward children.

1. (10:2) *What question did the Pharisees direct to Jesus?*

2. (10:3-5) *Jesus did not fall into the trap of answering the Pharisees directly. Rather, He asked them to quote Moses and then He explained God's plan. Why had Moses given guidelines on how to handle divorce?*

❒ *How might someone today demonstrate "hardness of heart"?*

3. (10:6–9) *What did Jesus tell them about marriage as God meant it to be?*

4. (10:10-12) *Since God has joined the husband and wife, what is the consequence of divorce and remarriage?*

5. (10:13-16) *Why would the disciples rebuke those who brought children to Jesus?*

❒ *How are little children an example to us?*

THE PROBLEMS OF TRUSTING IN WEALTH (Mark 10:17–31)

Every one of us has inner drives that motivate us. The rich young man claimed to be concerned with eternity. But it became apparent that he chose to trust wealth above faith and cling to it instead of to Jesus Christ.

1. (10:17–23) *What observations and conclusions can you draw about the rich young man's motives, attitudes, desires?*

❐ *Externally, this man seemed to be sincere, but what did he hope would enable him to receive eternal life?*

2. (10:21) *What was the "one thing" the man lacked for eternal life? What would obedience to Jesus' instructions have demonstrated about the man's faith?*

3. (10:24-25) *What illustration did Jesus give to explain how trusting in riches conflicts with trusting in Him?*

4. (10:26-31) *How did Jesus answer the question, "Who then can be saved?"*

❐ *Contrast Jesus' servant-values with the values His disciples (and many people today) placed on things.*

THE FUTURE AND OUR ATTITUDES (Mark 10:32-45)

Even though Jesus was very explicit in warning His disciples of the coming sorrows, they still were jockeying for position. He had to take time out to reinforce the message that spiritual leadership comes through service, not position.

1. (10:33–34) *What events did Jesus say would occur after He and His disciples reached Jerusalem?*

2. (10:37) *James and John had just heard Jesus tell them about His imminent death. Yet, they were still self-absorbed. What honor did James and John want Jesus to bestow upon them?*

3. (10:38–39) *What did Jesus mean when He spoke about drinking His cup and being baptized with His baptism? (See also verses 33-34.)*

4. (10:42) *Gentile is a general term that often referred to those who operated on the basis of an earthly, physical value system rather than by God's values and principles. What did Jesus say was the attitude of Gentiles as they led and directed others?*

5. (10:43–45) *What lessons of a servant heart does Jesus give here?*

❒ *How was Jesus an example of the principles that He taught in this passage?*

JESUS HEALS BARTIMAEUS (Mark 10:46–52)

*E*ven though Jesus' encounter with the blind beggar Bartimaeus seemed to be an incidental encounter, it presents a significant contrast to the attitudes of the Pharisees and the rich young man. Bartimaeus knew who Jesus was and he demonstrated his faith.

1. (10:46-51) *What was Bartimaeus' attitude toward Jesus and toward those who were around him? (Notice especially the names he uses in addressing Jesus.)*

2. (10:52) *What did Jesus say was the reason Bartimaeus was healed?*

DIGGING DEEPER

1. *Based on Jesus' explanation of marriage, how can we support God's ideal and, at the same time, be sensitive and compassionate to those who have fallen short of this ideal?*

2. *The rich young man's declaration of perfect obedience (10:20) was presumptuous. His attitude toward money revealed that he had broken the very first commandment (Exodus 20:3). How could wealth and possessions hinder us from trusting in Jesus and from following Him?*

❐ *What should our attitude be toward our material assets?*

3. *Much like Solomon's prayer for wisdom instead of riches, Bartimaeus went straight to the point of the best gift he could receive. What does this reflect about his faith?*

❐ *How does yours compare?*

❐ *How is such commitment reflected in your value system and the way you view material possessions?*

4. *Think about those with whom you might experience a power struggle. Why do you think you have conflict over who is in charge or have difficulty supporting them wholeheartedly?*

❐ *How do you think the relationship might change if you were to take a servant attitude?*

❐ *How does Jesus' attitude provide a good example for you?*

❖

Triumphal Entry and Rejection

MARK 11:1—12:44

❖

Recently we watched a bit of the baseball "old-timers" game. The commentators attempted valiantly to speak positive, encouraging words about the ex-stars as they ineptly fielded baseballs, tried to connect at the plate, or lumbered around the bases. But it was obvious from their comments and from the half-hearted cheers of the fans that at best it was an exercise in nostalgia. These players—the best of the best in their prime—are has-beens. Once they were cheered wildly. Now they are viewed with polite amusement.

No one is more keenly aware of the temporary nature of fame than athletes. An athlete may perform amazing feats in competition, break records, and lead the home team to victory. But watch what happens when that person's skills decline, or when someone with more skill arrives on the scene. The fans soon boo the previous hero and clamor for bigger and better things.

A similar phenomenon accompanied Jesus' ministry. But it had nothing to do with any change in Jesus. His loss of popularity rested solely in the fickleness of those who claimed to follow Him. The religious leaders had viewed Jesus as a threat from their earliest encounters. They should have been expecting the Messiah and evaluating Jesus' ministry based on the messianic prophecies. Instead, they tried to find any possible flaws. And when they could find none, they manufactured some. After repeated attempts to entrap, discredit, and confuse Him, the leaders finally succeeded in turning the people against Him. And the fickle public fulfilled the precise role the religious leaders had hoped they would.

On Sunday it was, "Hosanna! Blessed is He who comes in the name of the Lord." On Thursday, "Crucify Him!" And all of this played a part in the unfolding drama of redemption.

Throughout the book of Mark, we see intense and growing conflict between Jesus and the Jewish religious leaders who stood in opposition to Him. This conflict seems to reach a climax in chapters 11 and 12. At this point, Jesus' ministry was drawing rapidly to a close. In order to understand who these leaders were and why there was such conflict, let's identify the key protagonists.

Sadducees: These were wealthy Jewish leaders who wielded great power in the Jewish community. They were humanistic in their approach, rejecting the idea of the resurrection, eternal judgment, angels, and supernatural intervention.

Chief Priests: Temple leaders were chosen from the sect of the Sadducees. And while the chief priests strongly promoted and nurtured religious ritual, it was more of a business than a spiritual activity.

Elders: Lay leaders were chosen to work closely with and assist the priests in the temple. Sometimes they were selected from among the Pharisees. Elders played an important role in the Council of Seventy (the Sanhedrin), as did representatives from the other religious sects.

Pharisees: These were the rigid, meticulous legalists. Pharisees were vitally concerned with the study and interpretation of the Mosaic Law. But far beyond that, they spent much time studying, debating, and formalizing additional detailed regulations passed along by word of mouth. It was this group that demanded precise obedience to real or imagined laws, so that the Jews were totally oppressed by the ritualistic legal requirements. Unfortunately, few of them cared about the spirit of the Mosaic Law, and they often contradicted the spirit through the letter of the Law.

Scribes: Some of the Pharisees were called Scribes (often referred to as "teachers of the law"). These were Pharisees who wrote down details of legal requirements and taught them to others. Since they were teachers, they often were called Rabbi, a name they loved to hear.

Lawyers: These were Pharisees who studied and debated the theoretical aspects of the law. They were not lawyers in the present-day sense of attorneys, but rather students of religious law.

JESUS' TRIUMPHAL ENTRY (Mark 11:1–11)

Many have found that fame is a fleeting thing. And yet few heroes who receive public acclaim ever were dropped the way Jesus was. In this passage He is praised and adored as the Messiah. But in five short days, many of the same crowd will clamor for His crucifixion.

1. (11:1–6) *How are these events a fulfillment of prophecy in Zechariah 9:9?*

❒ *What does the response of the colt's owner say about the certainty of biblical prophecy?*

2. (11:7–10) *From your observation of verses 7– 10, describe how the people received Jesus.*

3. (11:11) *Why do you think Jesus went first to the temple when He entered Jerusalem?*

JESUS CLEANSES THE TEMPLE (Mark 11:12–26)

On the day after the Triumphal Entry (Palm Sunday), Jesus entered the temple again and found a mess. We can be sure that the fury of the Son of God was unlike any ever seen before. And in terror the merchandisers abandoned their lucrative trade.

1. (11:12–14) *Fig trees produce edible buds before they produce leaves, and after the leaves they produce figs. If there were no edible buds by the time the leaves had appeared, no figs would grow later. Why would Jesus include this episode with the barren fig tree? What might it symbolize?*

2. (11:15–17) *A market had been set up in the outer court of the temple (the court of the Gentiles) to sell sacrificial items and to exchange money. Why did Jesus respond so intensely in the temple area?*

❒ *What should the temple have been and what had it become?*

3. (11:18) *How did the religious leaders respond to Jesus' actions in the temple courtyard?*

4. (11:20–26) *The fig tree which bore no fruit symbolizes the Jewish nation which rejected Jesus as Messiah. Note how Jesus answered Peter's comment. Why would He relate prayer to this event?*

❒ *Are verses 23-24 a guarantee that we can ask God for anything and expect to get what we want?*

❒ **(11:25)** *What else is needed besides a proper relationship with God if we expect Him to answer our prayers?*

RELIGIOUS LEADERS CONFRONT JESUS (Mark 11:27—12:12)

Anyone who has tried to answer questions before an audience knows how difficult it can be. And yet, even though the shrewdest of the religious leaders combined their efforts, Jesus parried their attacks and cut their logic to ribbons.

1. (11:27–28) *The leaders of what three religious groups confronted Jesus?*

❒ *What was their initial question?*

2. (11:29–32) *What question did Jesus ask the leaders?*

❒ *Why could they not answer His question?*

3. (12:1–11) *A parable is "an earthly story with a heavenly meaning," or "an extended metaphor." It has meaning on the obvious, literal level, but the elements also represent another, spiritual meaning. It is most important in interpreting a parable to look only for the general spiritual message and not expect to* *find exact parallels in every detail of the account. The meaning of this parable becomes obvious when the characters in it are identified. Whom do each of the characters in this parable represent?*

Vineyard owner —

Husbandmen (hired farmers) —

Servant —

Other servants —

Son —

4. (12:12) *What do you think the religious leaders understood the parable to mean?*

❐ *What was their response?*

RELIGIOUS LEADERS TRY TO TRAP JESUS (Mark 12:13–27)

*I*f politics makes strange bedfellows, then religious politics generates even stranger alliances. Three of the most unlikely groups combined their efforts to trap Jesus in their logical, verbal battles. And each time Jesus turned the tables, the religious leaders became more vehement in their opposition.

1. (12:13) *This is a political alliance between the Herodians (pro–Roman rule) and the Pharisees (opposed to the Romans) who hated each other, but came together to oppose a common enemy. What was the purpose of the Pharisee/Herodian alliance?*

2. (12:14-17) *How did the religious leaders try to play up to Jesus and try to lead Him into a trap through flattery?*

❒ *How did Jesus avoid the trap and place the burden back on the conspirators?*

3. (12:18–23) *The Sadducees were anti-supernaturalists who rejected the ideas of both the resurrection and eternal judgments. Summarize the situation presented by the Sadducees by which they hoped to trap Jesus.*

4. (12:24–27) *How did Jesus turn the trap around to ensnare the Sadducees?*

JESUS CONCLUDES THE CONFRONTATION (Mark 12:28–44)

We often hear that one rotten apple spoils the entire barrel. Unfortunately, it doesn't work in reverse. By the time Jesus' opponents were silenced, the one questioner who seemed sincere addressed Jesus. And Jesus' response to his sincerity was one of encouragement. It's too bad that this one didn't influence the others.

1. (12:28) *This is one of the few times when a Pharisee is seen in a positive light. Either very few were this sincere, or else those who were kept a very low profile. Why did this man ask Jesus his question?*

❐ *What was the question from this teacher of the law?*

2. (12:29–31) *How did Jesus respond to this question?*

3. (12:32-33) *What does the scribe's response say about his knowledge of the Old Testament and God?*

4. (12:34) *Why do you think that no one dared to ask Jesus any more questions after this confrontation?*

5. (12:35–37) *In Jewish understanding, the elder always deserves more honor than his descendant. Which descendant of David did Jesus question the people about?*

❐ *What did the fact that David called an earthly descendant "Lord" support and illustrate?*

❐ *The false religious leaders (the intellectuals of the day) rejected Jesus, but the common people "heard him gladly." What parallels can you draw between Jesus' reception then and today?*

6. (12:38–40) *What warnings did Jesus give about false religious leaders?*

7. (12:41–44) *What is the obvious contrast between the poor woman and the wealthy contributors, other than the actual amounts they gave?*

❒ *In what sense did she give more than any of the others?*

DIGGING DEEPER

1. *What guidelines should we follow in the way that we pray, and what consequences should we expect as a result of praying?*

2. *Who are some false religious leaders today?*

❒ *How should we respond to them?*

3. *Compare Jesus' teaching (12:15–17) about recognizing dual accountability (to government and to God) with Paul's later teaching in Romans 13:1–7. Summarize the guidelines that we should follow.*

My accountability to:	***Government***	***GOD***
Mark 12:15-17		
Romans 13:1-7		

4. *How should our love for God affect the way that we use our resources and the attitude with which we give to God (12:43–44)?*

10

Jesus' Preparation for His Death

MARK 13:1—14:26

❖

Several years ago friends of ours experienced the loss of both of the wife's parents in a tragic automobile accident while the parents were traveling on vacation. Our friends grieved over this loss, but knew that both parents were prepared to meet God. They had lived full lives of service for God and were anxiously awaiting the privilege of meeting their Saviour.

Our friends went to the parents' home to care for whatever matters required attention there. They knew that the mother had been a careful housekeeper, but they were totally unprepared for the sight that greeted them as they entered the parents' home. Absolutely everything was in place. As a matter of fact, the home was so well prepared that it appeared the mother knew she would never return.

Imagine our friends' surprise when they noticed that the mother had placed little notes all over the house. She identified what should be done with each item in case they did not return. This reinforced in our friends' minds that the parents also were prepared spiritually to leave this life.

Jesus was keenly aware of the fact that His time on earth was virtually at an end, and He had told those who were closest to Him. But for the most part, they seemed insensitive to what He said. The religious leaders were plotting to execute Him—and they would succeed. Whether she understood fully or not, one woman helped to prepare Jesus for His burial. By anointing Him with costly perfume, she not only demonstrated her love and devotion, but she also helped to prepare Him for the agonizing trip to the cross.

WARNINGS TO JESUS' FOLLOWERS (Mark 13:1–11)

Most of us marvel at great architectural achievements. The disciples were no different. But Jesus encouraged His followers to turn from the physical and temporal to think about the coming events that would affect both them and all other believers, either directly or indirectly.

1. (13:1-2) *What was wrong with the disciples' focusing their attention on the physical building?*

2. (13:3–4) *What two questions did the disciples ask Jesus privately?*

3. (13:5–6) *What warning did Jesus give to His disciples to encourage them to be alert spiritually?*

4. (13:7–8) *What events will take place in the world between Jesus' crucifixion and His second coming?*

5. (13:9-11) *There is a difference in intensity between the kind of persecution that the disciples experienced and the Great Tribulation that is yet to come. What trials and persecutions would the disciples experience after Jesus left them?*

❒ *What did Jesus say the disciples' attitude should be toward the future problems that they would encounter?*

❒ *What mission would they fulfill in spite of persecution?*

EXPLANATION ABOUT THE END OF THE AGE (Mark 13:12–23)

The problems that the disciples encountered in the first century were quite mild compared to the worldwide Tribulation still to come. Jesus described what those going into the Tribulation will experience, and the fact that even then they would not be forsaken by God.

1. (13:14–19) *The abomination of desolation is a reference to a time during the Tribulation when the Anti-christ will try to establish himself in place of Jesus. What did Jesus want His readers to understand about this period? What will happen?*

2. (13:20) *"The elect" refers to Jews who turn to Christ during the Tribulation. What would have happened if God had not sovereignly limited the duration of the Tribulation?*

3. (13:21–23) *What will false prophets promise during this period?*

JESUS' SECOND COMING (Mark 13:24–37)

Although the events of the Tribulation will be terrible, they will conclude with a glorious event. Jesus will return to the earth as was prophesied in the Old Testament and as He promised His followers while He was on the earth with them.

1. (13:24–26) *What does this physical description of the events of the Tribulation sound like to you?*

❐ *According to these verses, what will Christ's return be like?*

What similarities or differences do you see in this description of Jesus' Second Coming with His first coming to earth?

	Similarities	*Differences*
Birth		
Second Coming		

2. (13:28–33) *"This generation" refers to those who are alive when the indicator events (verses 14–23) occur on the earth. What promises of Jesus do you see in these verses?*

❒ *What should you think when someone gives a date for the Rapture of the church or the Second Coming of Christ?*

3. (13:34-37) *Christ gave us another parable in these verses. How does this apply to believers awaiting Jesus' return?*

❒ *What should we be doing on the basis of this exhortation?*

JESUS ANOINTED FOR DEATH (Mark 14–1:11)

Preparation for burial was an involved, ritualistic procedure—more so in the first century than today. But for Jesus, there would be no opportunity, so God sent a woman to anoint Him ahead of time. The more materialistic disciples felt that it was a waste, and yet Jesus commended the woman for her act of devotion.

1. (14:1–2) *The attitude of the religious leaders directly reflected their response to Jesus' growing popularity and their antagonism toward Him described in Mark 11 and 12. They wanted to kill Him. Why were they hesitant to follow through on their intentions?*

2. (14:3-9) *The events of Mark 14:3–9 had occurred earlier but are reported here to develop Mark's theme. What happened to Jesus and why was it important? Contrast Jesus' attitude with the disciples' attitude toward His being anointed with perfume.*

Jesus ***Disciples*** ***Importance***

❒ *What was Jesus' promise about the woman's outpouring of love?*

3. (14:10–11) *This picks up the chronological flow from verse 2 and relates events leading up to Jesus' crucifixion. What action did Judas take? How did the religious leaders respond?*

THE LAST SUPPER WITH THE DISCIPLES (Mark 14:12–26)

It is no accident that Jesus was crucified at the time of the Passover, the annual ceremonial dinner commemorating God's deliverance of Israel from Egypt, and the passing over of the death angel. (See Exodus 12:1–20.) But at this Passover, the perfect Lamb that would be slain was the Son of God. Even as Jesus shared in this Passover dinner, He explained that it was His body and His blood that was being offered for the disciples' sins and the sins of the world.

1. (14:12–16) *Notice the detail given in this account for where the Last Supper should take place. It had been planned since before the foundation of the world. What events took place on the day before Jesus' death as the disciples prepared the Passover dinner?*

2. (14:17–18) *What did Jesus' startling announcement reveal about Him?*

3. (14:19-21) *How did the disciples react to this announcement?*

❐ *Matthew 26:25 recounts that Jesus told Judas (privately) that he was the one. How do you think Jesus felt about Judas and the coming events?*

4. (14:22–24) *What is the symbolic meaning of the bread and the wine with which Jesus and His disciples finished the meal?*

DIGGING DEEPER

1. *The prophecy that the temple would be destroyed and each stone knocked down (13:2) was fulfilled at Jerusalem's destruction in AD 70. What beautiful things are part of our worship of God but could, inappropriately, usurp His place and become our focus?*

2. *Compare Mark 13:11 with Jesus' promise in John 14:16–17, 26 to send the Holy Spirit (the Comforter) to be with His disciples. What do these verses say to you about your resources to face difficult circumstances?*

3. *What kinds of difficulties should we be prepared to encounter as followers of Christ, and what part do we play in proclaiming the gospel to all nations?*

4. *Many churches seem to have adopted Jesus' words in the Upper Room for their celebration of the Lord's Supper communion. (Compare I Corinthians 11:23–26.) What should be our attitude, approach, and response when we celebrate the Lord's Supper today?*

5. *How might you deny (betray) Jesus in your everyday actions?*

❐ *How do you think Jesus feels when we deny Him, and how do you think He responds to us when we do?*

❖

Jesus' Arrest and Trial

MARK 14:27—15:20

❖

For many years, one of the TV network sports shows has begun with the motto, "The thrill of victory and the agony of defeat." One of their best representations of the agony of defeat is an athlete skiing down a slope for a long-distance jump. Just before the take-off, the unfortunate athlete lost control and slipped off the side of the jump. His inglorious conclusion, as he sprawled into the bystanders, has been documented week after week, season after season, year after year.

Perhaps this nameless athlete was an extremely competent ski jumper. He might have been worried, or ill, or just unfortunate on that particular day. He may never have experienced such an incident before or after that day. And yet that particular event is recorded clearly and dramatically for all to view, week after agonizing week.

Some have theorized that failure is far less demoralizing than the knowledge that others are aware of that failure. And those who are in the limelight must deal with the fact that whatever they do may well become public knowledge. In recent years we have seen the flaws, foibles, and outright sins of national sports, political, and religious leaders. Former President Ford, one of our most athletic presidents, was captured by the camera in an unfortunate stumble. And forever many will think of him as a klutz.

Both Peter and Judas are remembered for bad decisions they made under pressure. But there is a difference in how they handled their errors. Peter obviously grieved over his mistake, but returned to Jesus and experienced a life of great fruitfulness. Judas, on the other hand, went out and committed suicide (Matthew 27:3–5). May we learn and profit from their experiences.

JESUS' AGONY IN GETHSEMANE (Mark 14:27–42)

How do you feel when those closest to you—those on whom you rely—let you down? That was what Jesus experienced in Gethsemane. Just when Jesus most needed His friends to stand with Him, they fell asleep, and He agonized alone.

1. (14:27) *Jesus' omniscience is clearly evident again in these verses. After Jesus and the remaining 11 disciples walked about a mile across the Kidron Valley to the Mount of Olives, what did Jesus say His disciples would do in the near future?*

2. (14:29-31) *Why did Peter receive Jesus' special notice of failure when all of them said they would not deny Him?*

3. (14:32–33) *Gethsemane is a secluded place at the foot of the northwest slope of the Mount of Olives. Whom did Jesus take with Him into the Garden?*

4. (14:35–36) *"Abba," the word Jesus used here to address God, was a little child's term of endearment similar to "Daddy." What emotions and attitudes are evident in Jesus' prayer?*

5. (14:37-42) *In these verses, what was happening to Jesus?*

❐ *To the disciples?*

❐ *What application do Jesus' words in verse 38 have for you today?*

ARREST AND TRIAL BEFORE THE SANHEDRIN (Mark 14:43–65)

A stealthy approach under cover of darkness, confrontation in a wooded area, betrayal by a double agent, and trial before a kangaroo court. Jesus' arrest had all the elements of a modern spy thriller. And yet this was not fiction. Jesus, the Son of God, was the key figure in a drama—not of international intrigue, but of redemption. But the case against Jesus was so weak that even the "purchased witnesses" couldn't agree. It was Jesus' own statement, affirming that He was God's Son, that provided what Caiaphas wanted—an accusation of blasphemy, punishable by death.

1. (14:43) *The crowd sent from the Sanhedrin (the highest Jewish court, with representatives from the priests, Pharisees, and elders) included Roman soldiers. What kind of response did the crowd apparently expect from Jesus and the disciples?*

2. (14:44–45) *Why was Judas's method of betrayal particularly poignant?*

3. (14:47–52) *Many scholars think that Mark, the author of this Gospel, was the young man following Jesus who fled. What was Jesus' response to the events unfolding around Him?*

4. (14:53–65) *When the soldiers led Jesus away, the conspiracy by Jesus' enemies had finally reached the point of success. Describe the trial before the high priest. (You may want to draw the courtroom and label those present as if in a modern trial.) Who were the witnesses? How credible was their testimony? What did the Chief Witness, Jesus, say? What did the chief accusers say? Who delivered the verdict? What truths and falsehoods were told? What evidence was there for conviction and a verdict of innocent?*

PETER'S DENIAL OF JESUS (Mark 14:66–72)

Anyone who has made, and then failed to keep, New Year's resolutions ought to empathize with Peter. He wanted to do what was right, even to the point of vowing to be faithful—forever. But he was human and discovered that human strength failed him when he most wanted to be strong. And we all are cut from the same cloth as Peter.

1. (14:66–70) *Confronted by two female servants, why would Peter feel intimidated enough to lie to them and the others around him?*

❐ *How did Peter attempt to prove that he was not one of Jesus' followers?*

2. (14:71-72) *How do you think Peter felt when he recalled Jesus' prediction made earlier in the evening? (As if remembering Jesus' words weren't enough, Luke 22:61 records that Peter observed Jesus looking down at him.)*

JESUS' TRIAL BEFORE PILATE (Mark 15:1–20)

Why go through the mockery of a second trial when the outcome already had been determined? While the Sanhedrin could find a person guilty, only the Roman authorities could sentence to death.

1. (15:1-10) *What is the scene in these verses?*

• *What were the questions asked of Jesus?*

• *What was Jesus' response? Why?*

• *What did Pilate think of the evidence and the trial? What did he want to do? (See also John 19:12; Luke 23:14-17.)*

• *Apparently to create good will, Pilate released a prisoner (possibly political) at Passover time. Why would Pilate have thought that the people wanted him to release Jesus to them?*

2. (15:11–15) *Why did Pilate finally condemn Jesus to death?*

3. (15:16–20) *These actions foreshadow the day when everyone ultimately will worship the name of Jesus (Philippians 2:9–11). What did the soldiers do to Jesus?*

DIGGING DEEPER

1. *In what situations might we face conflict between what we feel like doing and what we know we ought to do?*

❒ *How can we resolve such conflict appropriately?*

2. *In what ways can Jesus serve as an example to us as we observe how He responded to being abandoned by His friends and misrepresented and abused by His enemies?*

3. *Before condemning Peter for his failure, we ought to ask where the other disciples were. At least Peter was nearby. How does Jesus' lack of condemnation, and His later encouragement of Peter (John 21:15–19) encourage you?*

4. *How does Pilate's strategy for resolving the conflict between public pressure and personal conscience serve as a warning to all of us?*

❖

Jesus' Victory Over Death

MARK 15:21—16:20

❖

Many of us spend some time in "do-it-yourself" activities. One motivation may be to economize. Knowing how expensive it is to hire a skilled craftsman, we look at a project that doesn't appear too difficult and ask, "Why not just do it myself?"

Others take on projects for the enjoyment of working with their hands. We look for challenging tasks, sometimes spending many hours working on one project. And success increases motivation to attempt new and greater things.

Whichever the reason—to save money or because of the challenge—at one time or another most of us have found ourselves in over our heads. The project that looked so simple at the outset has become a complex nightmare.

The parts that should have come apart easily, don't. And the replacement part that we were sure would fit, doesn't. So we find ourselves stymied and frustrated. It seems as though no matter what we try, we are no closer to our goal than when we started.

Multiply that discouragement and frustration many times and you can understand how the Jewish leaders in Jesus' time may have felt. Jesus had been a constant irritation to the religious leaders. After trying to discredit Him in a variety of ways, they finally resorted to deception. Even collaboration with the Roman authorities was acceptable if they could have Him executed. And they succeeded—or so they thought. But their problems had only begun. Because now Jesus was alive forever, resurrected! Any problems they had before would pale into insignificance.

CRUCIFIXION OF JESUS (Mark 15:21–32)

Most authors and speakers who address the topics of leadership and management stress the importance of setting clear, specific goals. Jesus' entire ministry on earth was directed toward the time that He would be called on to die and conquer both sin and death. This was His goal, and He moved relentlessly toward it.

1. (15:21–22) *Ordinarily a victim carried his own cross (probably weighing about 100 pounds). It also symbolized that the Romans were justified in sentencing you to death. What is the symbolic meaning of Golgotha?*

2. (15:23) *Why do you think that Jesus refused the pain-deadening wine mixed with myrrh?*

3. (15:21–32) *Read through the prophecies in Psalm 22:11–18 and make a list of the prophetic statements that you find fulfilled in these verses.*

Psalm 22 Prophecy	*Mark 15 Fulfillment*

4. (15:26) *What is ironic about the statement of Jesus' "offense" written on the sign posted on Jesus' cross?*

5. (15:27–32) *What were the attitudes of those around Jesus as He was crucified?*

6. (15:31–32) *In spite of what the mockers said, Jesus obviously could have saved Himself had He so chosen. Why didn't He?*

DEATH AND BURIAL OF JESUS (Mark 15:33–47)

Many people were crucified by the Romans, and they died with many different attitudes. Some died cursing while others died pleading. Some died screaming in pain. But no one died in the way that Jesus did. When He had finished the task before Him, He dismissed His own spirit—and died. He was in control; He was the victor. And we live because of it.

1. (15:33–39) *What five events does Mark record that occurred as Jesus was dying?*

1.

2.

3.

4.

5.

2. (15:33) *What might be the reason for darkness from noon to 3 p.m. (the sixth to the ninth hours) as Jesus was hanging on the cross?*

3. (15:34) *Jesus' cry is a quote from Psalm 22:1. Why was it necessary for God to turn His back on Jesus as He was dying? (See also Psalm 88:14-16 and II Corinthians 5:21.)*

4. (15:38) *The curtain of the temple was a heavy tapestry, separating the holy place from the most holy place where the high priest offered the yearly sacrifice for Israel's sin. What is the significance of Mark's pointing out that this curtain was torn in half from the top down?*

5. (15:39) *What conclusion did the Roman centurion reach about Jesus? What do you think led the centurion to this conclusion?*

6. (15:42–47) *What can you conclude about Joseph of Arimathea, a member of the Sanhedrin, from Mark's description of the events surrounding Jesus' burial?*

RESURRECTION OF JESUS (Mark 16:1–8)

Jesus told His disciples on several occasions that He would rise from the dead. But when it actually took place, everyone seemed surprised.

1. (16:1-3) *Why did women come to the tomb? Where were the disciples? (See also Matthew 28:1–10; Luke 24:1–12, and John 20:1–18.)*

❒ *Why did they come if they thought the tomb would be sealed?*

2. (16:4–7) *What important facts of the miracle of the resurrection are given in these verses?*

❒ *What did the angel tell the women who entered the tomb?*

3. (16:8) *Eventually they notified the disciples, but what did the women do initially?*

CONCLUDING EVENTS (Mark 16:9–20)

The writing style and vocabulary in these verses are quite different from Mark's, indicating that he probably didn't write this section himself. It is possible that another disciple added it sometime after the Gospel was finished. But it was received and accepted by the early church as the correct conclusion to the Gospel.

1. (16:9–14) *To what persons or groups did Jesus appear, and what were their responses?*

Person/Group	***Response***

2. (16:15–16) *What mission did Jesus give to His disciples?*

3. (16:17–18) *What miraculous signs did Jesus indicate would accompany their preaching? (These particular miraculous signs were addressed to the disciples and should not be assumed to apply to all believers.)*

4. (16:19-20) *How did Jesus conclude His ministry on earth at His first coming?*

DIGGING DEEPER

1. *Jesus died so that we can be saved from our sin and receive eternal life. We need only to accept His free gift of salvation. If you have accepted Jesus as your Saviour, write a brief prayer of thanksgiving. If you have not yet accepted Jesus' offer but would like to, ask Jesus now to be your Saviour. Then write a brief prayer stating that you accept salvation and thank God for it.*

2. *Romans 5:6–11 very clearly teach that Jesus' sacrificial death is the means by which each individual may receive the free gift of salvation. What impact should it have when you realize that Jesus willingly sacrificed Himself for you?*

3. *It was obvious that Jesus was in control at every step, even to the point of dismissing His spirit when He was ready to die. (See John 19:28–30.) How does this add to the meaning of His victorious death and its implications for you personally?*

4. *Joseph and the women showed their devotion to Jesus tangibly. How can you express your devotion to Jesus today?*

5. *What acts of service do you think Jesus expects from you as you follow Him today? Make a list of specific things that you think Jesus would have you do. Select one of them and ask God to help you to fulfill it.*

6. *As the book of Mark ends, how do you see verses 19-20 carrying out the theme of the Servant-Saviour?*

❐ *Look back over the book of Mark. List the major points, truths, or events that show Jesus as the Servant-Saviour.*

❐ *How can you apply these lessons on servanthood to your life and become more Servant-like?*

❖